Ultimate GRACE

Ultimate GRACE

A true story of Frisbee and faith in Japan

Levi Booth

First published in Great Britain in 2019, reprinted once.

British Library Cataloguing in Publication Data
A record for this book is available from the British Library

ISBN: 978-1-912373-67-3

Designed and typeset by Pete Barnsley (CreativeHoot.com)

Printed in Denmark by Nørhaven

10Publishing, a division of 10ofthose.com
Unit C, Tomlinson Road, Leyland, PR25 2DY, England

Email: info@10ofthose.com
Website: www.10ofthose.com

Contents

Foreword

The only way to live the Christian life is to be gripped by grace. Levi Booth came to realise this fact as a teenager and it led him to a life he did not plan. But it was a life he would never give up.

In this short book, Levi shares his story of how God used different people and a variety of experiences to shape his life and prepare him for a unique mission. How could a love of Ultimate Frisbee, Jackie Chan and *anime* possibly come together and be used by God to help spread the gospel? *Ultimate Grace* shows that whatever your situation, or whatever your passions, God can use them to fulfil his own gospel purpose.

As you read it, I pray you will be moved, blessed and, most of all, challenged to discover something of the wonder of God's grace. Grace which is for everyone – even through missed opportunities, trials and hardships. And I pray it might help you think about how you could use the situations, passions and gifts that God has given you for his purpose and glory.

Chris Pain,
Field Director OMF Japan

Introduction

My feet were burning. I didn't know sand could get this hot. I dug my feet into the slightly cooler sand underneath. But not too deep so that I'd still be able to run. I looked across the pitch to the opposition, the Great British team. I could see they were not nearly as exhausted as us, the Japanese Mixed Masters Ultimate Frisbee team. It was an odd feeling, lining up *against* Great Britain. I used to dream that I might one day play for them; I had never thought that I would end up playing against them. But I had no time to dwell on the unexpected journey that had led me here – representing Japan at the World Championships of Beach Ultimate – their puller raised the disc: the next point was about to start.

We were in Royan, a little beach town in western France. Doug, one of the other non-Japanese on the team, had found a cheap cottage for us to stay in. And the boy had done good. There was no Wi-Fi, but besides that it was five star luxury. If you can imagine the stereotypical French beachside cottage then you're probably imagining where we stayed. Except that for a cottage it was huge: six bedrooms, two showers, a beautiful wooden dining table big enough to sit us all and plenty of lounge floor space for post-game stretching and rolling.

And the kitchen ... for France it may have been fairly standard, but after four years of acclimatising to Japanese kitchens that are just about big enough for a two-ring gas hob and microwave (my rice cooker and kettle lived on a stand half-way into the dining room) it was breathtaking. There were pots and pans and utensils in abundance and more amazingly there was actual surface space to put them on!

But two things stood out above all, basking in the late-afternoon sun pouring through the French windows (although I guess in France they're just windows?): ovens. Two ovens. Not one oven with two sections, mind. Two whole ovens. And the farmers' market was just ten minutes walk away. On the way to France we had debated about whether it'd be better to do our own cooking or eat out, but now the right choice was obvious.

And so the night before the tournament began we gathered round the huge oak table to enjoy a meal of pasta, salad, cheese, bread, cold meats and more cheese (we may have got a bit carried away at the shops). In Japan it's customary before a meal to say together *itadakimas*. It literally means 'I receive this', but essentially is an expression of thankfulness and gratitude. I was waiting for the team captain to initiate the *itadakimas*, when one of the other members asked me, 'Hey Levi, why don't you pray for us?'

Before I could answer, I was met with a flurry of responses from everyone else.

'Yeah, do it! I've never heard a proper mealtime prayer before.'

'What's it called in English?'

'But why is Levi going to pray?'

'Don't you know? Levi's a pastor?'

'Seriously?'

'So is there a proper way we need to sit to pray?'

'Wait, wait, wait! You're really a pastor?'

'We have a team pastor! How cool is that!'

'Catholic? Or ... what's the other one?'

After we had established that yes, I really was a pastor, or, more accurately, a missionary, and that I was indeed happy to say a prayer, or grace, for the meal, I explained how people were free to close their eyes or keep them open and that it's traditional to end a prayer by everyone saying 'amen'.

And then I led us in a simple prayer of thanks for the food and for the opportunity to play Ultimate Frisbee together. I think for most of the team it was just a fun thing to do, but for me it was an utterly unexpected privilege and the beginning of an incredible week playing Ultimate Frisbee for Jesus with the Japanese national team. And between the games we hung out in this mansion of a cottage having banter about everything from reasons for staying single to the possibility of seeing spirits.

It'd been three years since I went out to Japan to start my first term as a full-time missionary. Three years of trying to work out how to fit in to Japan, what I should be doing and how, what it meant to be a missionary. Now I was starting to wonder whether it might all be as simple as me being me.

I'm guessing you've got a few questions about this whole scenario, one of the big ones being, 'So did you beat the British team?' The answer to that is, no. The answer to your other questions will, I hope, be found in the rest of this book.

1

From Frisbee –

OK so let's start with the big misconceptions.

Ultimate Frisbee does *not* involve dogs.

It's a team sport. Seven against seven. It's played on a pitch 100 metres long and 37 metres across with end zones at each end. It involves players passing around a regulation size and weight disc for 90 minutes or until one team has reached 15 points, scored by catching a pass into the end zone. It's kind of like a cross between American football and netball. It's ... not very easy to explain. Maybe it's best if you YouTube it.

Now I won't blame you for not knowing about Ultimate. The first time I heard about it my reaction was, 'Eh?'

I had just finished registering at university. With my newly printed student card in hand I entered the hall where all the sports clubs were waiting to recruit new members. I was planning on joining the *ju jitsu* club and maybe one other sport. Perhaps rugby. I had played a little bit at school and my natural nippiness had been useful.

I found out afterwards that the clubs were rotated round each year. By the time someone had walked through the whole hall they were a bit overwhelmed, so the spots near the entrance were highly sought after. That year Ultimate Frisbee had top spot, so I came through the door to discover a table covered in scratched-up Frisbees around a laptop playing some kind of highlight reel. I stood watching for a bit trying to work out what was going on. I frowned at the guy behind the table. He smiled back.

'Hi!'

'Hi. Er ... what?'

'Ultimate Frisbee.'

'Right.'

'Oh, check out this bit.'

He twisted the screen a bit so we could both see it. A Frisbee was flying through the air with someone running almost alongside it, a few feet behind, with a white line between them. It was obviously going to land the other side of the line, which I was guessing would be out of bounds. I was thinking of a polite way to say goodbye when suddenly the person running launched himself across the line going almost horizontal. He caught the Frisbee in his right hand, and almost in the same movement threw it whilst still in the air. The camera panned quickly down the line to a rectangle between four small orange cones. The Frisbee was about to land within the rectangle when another dude came diving into frame, snatching the Frisbee from the air before landing chest-first and sliding to a stop.

I had no idea what I had just watched. But I knew I wanted to be a part of it.

'They call that "a greatest".'

'Really?'

'First practice is this Saturday 10am at the pitches by Boddington Halls. Know where that is?'

I did. Those were the halls I lived in. I decided to go along and try out Ultimate Frisbee for myself.

I got the information about practices for rugby plus a few other cool-sounding sports. But after my first Frisbee practice, I knew this was the sport for me. I loved the energy of the game, the unpredictable nature of matches and above all I loved its ethos.

One of the defining features of Ultimate – and one that I continue to get flak for – is that it's a self-refereed sport. This means that players rely heavily on something called Spirit of the Game. It's broken down into five sections: understanding of the rules, self-control, fair play, positive attitude and communication. Or more simply, Spirit of the Game is about the two teams trusting each other. It's not so much that there's no referee in Ultimate, it's that *everyone* is a referee. And you know what? Somehow it works. If a foul is called, and the call is contentious, then that call is contested and the players chat it through until a decision is made and the game moves on. And then after the game, we high-five each other and sit down and give each other feedback. It's fun. It promotes sportsmanship and teamwork. It makes Ultimate Frisbee the sport it is, and over time it changes the people who play it. But, for me, in my first year at university, I was about to discover a spirit of a different kind.

2

– to Faith

Perhaps you feel a little like I did when I was a teenager? I had grown up going to church and thought that I had the whole Christian thing down. I had put my faith in Jesus and I knew I was going to heaven. I had also picked up that living like Jesus was the best way to be human. I wanted the fruit of the Spirit in my life. I could recite them from memory, along with the books of the Bible, and a whole bunch of Bible verses. I prayed before dinner. Most nights I prayed before I went to sleep. And I really believed that there was a God in heaven who was listening to my prayers.

But something was missing. I couldn't say 'no' to people. This became a problem when I made it to high school and all my friends wanted to go out drinking, clubbing and generally partying. I also lacked love. I was known as 'the nice guy' in my group of friends, but really all my plans revolved around me. I wanted to get a good degree, so I could get a good job, so I could get a nice house with a nice car and hopefully find a nice girl to marry and raise a nice family with. I'd enjoy a nice, long retirement and then go to heaven. As far as plans go, it seemed pretty watertight to me.

But at university my plan started to fall apart. And one of the reasons was a senior player on the Ultimate Frisbee team. I'll call him Steve – mostly because that's his name. One day I was talking to Steve and I must have said something about being a Christian or going to church, because he suggested we meet up to read the Bible together. This was a novel idea for me. I knew all about Sunday services in a church building, and I knew about youth groups on a Wednesday night at the home of a church member. But going to a café and just sitting down with a friend to read the Bible together without any fun stuff to pad out the time? I was intrigued. And also I really respected Steve. Even as a Frisbee newbie I could tell he was really good, and yet he was also humble and chilled out.

And so we started meeting together once a week to read through the book of 2 Timothy. I had read through the New Testament by myself, but never this slowly! I thought the point of reading the Bible was to – well to read the Bible. To get through it. But Steve seemed almost indifferent to whether we finished reading this letter to Timothy. He wanted me to think about what each verse meant, and he wanted to talk about why Paul had written it and what we were meant to do in response. We'd meet up in the café overlooking the student canteen each week, and sip coffee whilst chatting about the next couple of sentences.

To be honest, the first couple of weeks were a bit boring. Learning about Timothy's mum and grandma didn't really grab my attention. But when we reached 2 Timothy 1:7, where Paul writes that the 'Spirit God gave us does not make us timid, but gives us power, love and self-discipline' I was hooked. This was what I was missing. I *needed* this Spirit. But what did I have to do to get it?

I think it was the fourth or maybe fifth time meeting with Steve that we got to verse 9. I had of course heard about, and sung about, God's grace. But until now it had been something vague and undefined. I hadn't thought deeply about what it was. I didn't know you could, or should, think deeply about something like grace. But Steve pointed me to the end of the verse: 'This grace was given us in Christ Jesus before the beginning of time'. And then he asked me a very simple question that would change my life and set me on the course that has led me to be a missionary in Japan.

'If this is true, what does it mean for you?'

I had always assumed that my relationship with God was based partly on what I did. After all, that's how all my other relationships worked. If I got good grades, my teachers would praise me. If I made a funny joke, my friends would like me. Sure I knew my parents loved me unconditionally, but, well, they had to didn't they? How confident I felt of God's love for me at any time depended on how much I felt I had pleased him in the previous hours or days.

I guess up till then grace had kind of been like the Continue screen in computer games. I would go on by my own strength, eventually (or sometimes not so eventually) mess up, and then push the 'grace button' to reset my standing with God back to zero. It kept me confident enough that I would probably go to heaven if I were to actually die that day, but it was only after I'd built up enough points doing good deeds or general Christian stuff that I felt acceptable enough to approach God with anything like a degree of confidence.

I once heard someone say that God's grace is like a coin you put in a vending machine. Sometimes you have to give the machine a shake for the coin to properly drop. I read the verse again, took a sip of coffee, and read it once more. My eyes stopped on the final five words: 'before the beginning of time'. I felt my heart shake a little.

'If this grace was given to us before the beginning of time, then it can't have anything to do with what we've done. We don't earn it at all. It's 100 per cent totally free?'

I looked up at Steve. He was smiling.

'That's right.'

My heart shook again, stronger this time. Grace, finally, dropped.

3

The Cost of Discipleship

As Steve and I kept meeting up to read through the Bible I realised I had a choice. Carry on with my plans for a nice, comfortable life, or give up my plans to God and entrust myself to his free grace. I gave myself to reading through the Bible again. But this time not to earn points with God, but to get to know him. To learn what it actually meant to be a follower of Jesus Christ.

The problem was that although I had come to see that my plans weren't very well thought through – although I knew without a doubt that I wanted the sense of security and joy that people like Steve had – Jesus just seemed like quite an extreme sort of person. He just called to people in the midst of doing their jobs and told them, 'Follow me'. And then only after a couple of years of working miracles and teaching about the kingdom of heaven he mentioned that he was going to be wrongly arrested and publicly executed and that was all part of the plan. I'd heard Jesus' call to follow him and I knew he could be trusted with my life, but it was still pretty scary to let go of everything I was working towards.

Christians sometimes talk about having a key verse that they really feel has impacted their life. I'm not sure that I have one – the more I read the Bible, the more verses I find that I want to hold onto for life – but if I was made to choose, I'd probably go with Mark 10:28–30 (yeah, I know that's three verses, but the numbers are made up anyway, right?):

> *Then Peter spoke up, 'We have left everything to follow you!'*
>
> *'Truly I tell you,' Jesus replied, 'no one who has left home or brothers or sisters or mother or father or children or fields for me and the gospel*

> *will fail to receive a hundred times as much in this present age: homes, brothers, sisters, mothers, children and fields – along with persecutions – and in the age to come eternal life.'*

When I first read that passage, I was struck by how straightforward Jesus was. It seemed kind of crazy to me. I mean who would follow up a promise of repaying you one-hundred-times back for the people or stuff you give up for them with, 'Oh and also you'll face persecution'? To let people know there's going to be a huge cost in following you, you'd have to be super confident in your ability to make good on your promises and that they would outweigh the costs.

I think on some level I had always felt that uncertainty about Jesus' trustworthiness to make it worthwhile following him. My mum had for a few years gently pushed me about getting baptised, but I had dodged around the idea. Even when she promised to bake me a whole tray of millionaire's shortbread – to this day still my treat of choice – I couldn't be convinced to make a public confession of my faith.

But as I looked back on my life I was struck by how patient and faithful Jesus had been to me. I had treated him like a kind and rich, but odd, older brother. Someone I would go to for extra coins once I ran out at the arcade but then ignore until the next time I needed some. And yet he had never left me. I remembered all the answers to prayers I'd received, and realised there were undoubtedly a whole bunch more that I'd forgotten about in my ungrateful hurry to move on with my life. And in response Jesus had kept on calling me to come to him. Not for another boost of short-lived self-esteem and a vague hope of heaven, but for a life of totally-forgiven joy-filled adventure, starting now and continuing for eternity.

I mean, how was I meant to respond to that except to surrender everything to him?

At the time I had no idea of just what I'd be giving up to follow Jesus. But I knew I was potentially giving up all the things that Peter mentioned. And I had the feeling I would end up making the same complaint or comment to Jesus at least once during my life. But now I knew he would give me the same rebuke, reply and promise. So I took the plunge and got baptised.

And then almost as if he'd been waiting for this moment, God started to weave this new desire to follow Christ with an old interest of mine.

4
Kung Fu Kid

When I was in high school I had two heroes: Bruce Lee and Jackie Chan. But mostly Bruce Lee. (Yes, I know Bruce Lee is Chinese, not Japanese. I'm coming to that. Just chill for a minute.) I watched all his films over and over. I had posters of him doing that impossible-looking jumping kick, and one of him doing his famous 'hwahooo!' face with nunchucks tucked under one arm. I memorised his quotes: 'The art of fighting, without fighting'; 'Be like water'; 'The highest form is no form'. I had no idea what he meant – I still don't to be honest – but I knew I wanted to be like him.

One of my best friends was also into *kung fu*. We would go into town on Saturday to O'Harras

– a second-hand video store – and hunt through the shelves for any *kung fu* movies that had come in. Then rush home and watch whatever our latest find was, in awe of these dudes who could take on twelve men at once with their bare fists (or in Jackie Chan's case, a stepladder and a bucket). We decided that we needed to learn this *kung fu* stuff too.

But we lived in Warrington (a town once voted the 'least cultural city in Europe') and our options were limited. We went to the local sports centre, to see what classes they had on. There was one for something called *ju jitsu*. It sounded Asian and exotic enough. We signed up.

Turns out *ju jitsu* is a Japanese martial art, although our *senseis* (teachers) were from Bolton and Pakistan. But it didn't matter to me. I loved it, this 'art of gentleness'. Coming into the *dojo* (training hall) in my freshly ironed white *gi* (uniform). Bowing at the door and then again before getting onto the mat. The *sensei* inspecting my *obi* (belt) to see if it was tied properly. 'I'm not giving you a new belt if you're not going to tie it properly', was the frequent warning for anyone who tied theirs sloppily. Doing warm-up throws ('If you get attacked in the streets, you can't ask them to wait whilst you stretch') and seeing if you could make the CD player jump (the *sensei* had one CD of bad dance music, but we never dared ask him to change it).

And when we did gradings we were tested in the theory too. We had to learn the names of the bones in the body, basic first aid and the Japanese for things like throws, commands and counting. It was the beginning of my journey into Japanese language and culture.

About the same time I went round to visit my other best friend after school. His mum let me in and directed me upstairs. I knocked and went in. He was watching a cartoon, but not like any I'd seen before. It looked so realistic, even though, on the screen, I could see a girl riding on the back of a giant wolf.

'It's called *Princess Mononoke*,' he explained.

'Cool,' I responded (Adam and I had the deepest conversations), sitting down on the couch.

Even coming in half-way through the film and having no idea what was going on, I was enthralled. The art-style, the music, the story (what I understood of it) was unlike anything

I'd seen before (and I'd see all the Disney movies – even the straight to video stuff like *Aladdin 2: Return of Jafar*).

As we watched Princess Mononoke battle for the fate of her forest, Adam explained that this was an *anime* movie by someone called Hayao Miyazaki. Apparently he'd made a bunch of others like it. In the months that followed I hunted down as many as I could. As I did I also discovered samurai movies and other Japanese classics. I didn't give up on Bruce Lee or Jackie Chan, but now they shared my video collection with Studio Ghibli and Akira Kurosawa.

One day, I thought to myself, it'd be cool to go and visit Japan. I didn't know it then, but about the same time someone in Japan was thinking the same thing about visiting the UK. And I'm sure they weren't thinking about it either, but we were destined to meet and have a conversation that would push my thinking from 'go to visit' to 'give my life for'.

5

Realising the Need

Jump forward a few years to my baptism. It was a great day. My parents came over to watch. My mum came true on her promise to bake a whole tray of millionaire's shortbread. It was Baptist church, so we're talking full, full immersion. Utterly drenched I came out of the water smiling like an idiot. My nan held the towel for me and hugged me like only nan's can. I was totally pumped up and ready to change the world for Jesus.

But it turned out the world wasn't so eager to be changed. And I wasn't quite ready to be the one to bring change.

I tried to share the good news about Jesus with my friends. They were nice about it but mostly interested in what appeared to them to be more immediate issues like girls, grades, gigs and getting drunk.

I got involved with my Christian Union group, handing out flyers for lunchtime talks and even just going round the campus asking anyone sat down whether they wanted to talk about Jesus Christ. A few did. Most were just bemused. Some were angry. Some days I just got laughed at. I had expected people to be really interested in Jesus. He was, after all, the most incredible person I'd ever met. I couldn't understand why nobody was asking me to share with them his good news.

Until the day someone did.

It was during International Freshers Week. That's the week before Freshers week and two weeks before the start of the university term. The Christian Union had put up a big white tent – the kind you might use if you were having a fancy party in a garden, and if your garden was the size of a tennis court. We'd turned it into a make-shift café, and a pretty good one too. The tables were admittedly a bit shabby (they were these big round plastic tables that you couldn't move without one of the legs falling out). But there was a prayer corner with beanbags, cushions and a box of felt-tip pens and coloured paper. The lighting consisted of a random assortment of lamps that people had brought from their student flats, mixed with fairy lights that were mostly untangled. It was a football world-cup year and I had managed to convince one of the sports shops in town to give me the world flags from their window display. It looked cosy and inviting, in a slightly eccentric way.

I was taking my turn welcoming people who came into the tent. A couple of Asian-looking students walked in. I introduced myself, and asked them where they were from.

'Japan,' they answered.

Then one asked me what the tent was.

'It's a free café. We're the Christian Union, and we're welcoming students to Leeds.'

That's when it happened. The thing that I had thought I would never hear.

'Oh, so you're a Christian? I'm really interested in what Christians believe, but I don't know any Christians in Japan. Could you tell me about Christianity?'

'Erm ... yeah ... no, of course,' I replied, leading us to a spare table as I sent up a panicked prayer for help. I explained the basics of who Jesus is, what he's done, and what it means to be one of his followers. It wasn't the most gripping of deliveries and very soon I had totally lost one of the Japanese students, who wandered away to look at the flags. But the guy who had asked me the question was keen to listen and when I suggested coming along to the Bible studies we were running for international students, he happily agreed.

After a bit more talking he left, rescuing his friend from the flags and leaving me to ponder what had happened. I had assumed that Japan, being such an advanced country, wasn't the kind of place where you couldn't find someone to tell you about Jesus. I'd been reading about missionaries and from the books I'd read they all went to exotic, dangerous places where you had to be careful not to be eaten by the wildlife (or in some cases, the people) in order to share the gospel. Japan sounded much safer, more advanced and more comfortable than the UK. Could there be a need for missionaries to go to somewhere like Japan?

I did some research and discovered that yes, there was indeed a need. Even the most optimistic estimates suggested less than 1 per cent of the population were Christians. There were whole cities without a single known church. And most striking for me, as a member of a 150 member strong Christian Union, was finding out that as little as 0.002 per cent of Japanese students knew Jesus as their saviour. If my university, the University of Leeds, was in Japan, there'd be maybe three Christians in the entire university.

So now I knew that there was a need for missionaries to Japan, the question I needed to answer was: should I become one of them? I felt a growing concern for Japan. I had an interest in going and some understanding of the culture. But did I have a call from God to go, or was this just another one of my personal dreams?

I'm a fairly straightforward person so I decided the only way to know for sure was to go there and see what happened.

6
I Don't Have a Dream!

So after finishing university I went to Japan on a year-long Serve Asia short term mission trip with OMF. I was sent to a city called Sendai on the eastern coast. Now it's famous for being one of the cities worst affected by the 2011 tsunami, but at the time I was there it was simply a middle-sized city (by Japan standards) of roughly one million people. A mix of students, fishermen and jazz musicians (seriously, Sendai hosts one of Japan's largest jazz festivals, and in my completely underqualified opinion it's amazing).

I was linked up with a missionary couple to help with their outreach to students. I spent most of my year in Sendai helping with Bible studies at their house, hanging out with students on campuses, studying Japanese in Starbucks and encouraging Christian student groups.

But also I spent a lot of time praying on clifftops.

I prayed for a number of things, but mostly I prayed for two things: first, revival in Japan, and second, guidance for my future.

I prayed for these two things because I was feeling increasingly drawn to staying long-term in this beautiful, baffling country. I was constantly having my heart broken by stories of family breakdowns and work-induced burnouts, I knew students who were deeply interested in the claims of Christ but told me that they couldn't become a Christian 'because I'm Japanese'. And then I had Japanese Christian friends who were trying to get up the courage to tell their classmates that they went to church. I knew I wanted to do something to bring gospel freedom to Japan but I needed certainty that this was God's calling on my life.

So I prayed. I prayed for some kind of confirmation. A dream, or a vision, maybe just an audible voice. Something unmistakable. I prayed at home, on the train and as I walked around Sendai. And I prayed most of all on a cliff – the site of Sendai's castle ruins (which consisted of an outer wall and about eight half-buried stones). From there I could see almost all of the city. The International Center just below, the campus of Tohoku University next to that, Sendai train station with shopping malls sprawled all around it ahead of me and in the distance, off to the left, the 300 foot tall statue of Canon, the 'goddess of mercy', which overlooked the city. At night it became a sea of light. A million souls flickering before me, almost all of them walking in darkness without the hope of the gospel.

I prayed and prayed, and received no call. No vision, no dream, no voice.

Then one day in my daily Bible reading I read Acts 16:9–10. Paul saw a man of Macedonia calling him to take the gospel there and the church took that as a call from God to go. I realised then that whilst I didn't have a dream, I did have real-life Japanese people calling me to stay in Japan. Maybe the reason why God wasn't giving me a dream was because I didn't need one. Maybe God was calling me to Japan through his church.

I suggested this idea to OMF missionaries and my pastor in the UK. They responded with a kind of, 'well yeah obviously' confirmation. All I needed to do to confirm the call to life-long mission in Japan was graduate from Bible college, complete a bunch of interviews, pass a medical test, be commissioned by my church in Leeds, get my application accepted by OMF Japan and OMF UK and raise enough financial support for my first four year term in Japan.

But I also knew Jesus well enough by this point to be confident that if he was calling me to Japan, then he'd make a way for me to pass all those checkpoints. What I hadn't really appreciated was how many trials I would have to face after that.

7

Saying Goodbye and Other Trials

One of my best friends has a saying that he pulls out every time I mention finances: 'Money isn't the problem, it's the solution'. I think he's onto something with that, in fact I think you can go further: money is the means God uses to grow us. At least that was the case for me in the eight months it took to reach my funding target.

It wasn't really fun – scratch that, it was emphatically not fun. I came close to giving up a couple of times. It was months of wrestling with doubts, fighting self-pity and judgemental thinking and a fair bit of sulking at God. But through it all, God was teaching me about prayer, contentment, humility, persistence and above all he was training me to rest in him alone. As I slowly clued in to this I realised how this would equip me for my work in Japan, but some of those lessons would come into play before I left the UK.

If raising enough money for four years in Japan was tough, then leaving my family and friends was brutal. And especially leaving those people who would double in age before I saw them next.

There were four such people that I had to say goodbye to: Luke and Joel – my nephews – and Josh and Seth – my adopted nephews. I got to know Josh and Seth during my time at Bible college. Their parents, Pete and Katy, welcomed me into their family. Hanging out with them, and playing with Seth and Josh, helped make up for not seeing my real nephews so much. I had fun with both of them, but for whatever reason, Seth and I developed a special bond: he was my Seth-monster.

Seth was an unstoppable optimist. When I explained to him that going to Japan meant I wouldn't see him until he was seven, he happily announced that then he would simply turn seven at his next birthday. But I guess reality beat him. Pete told me that after I said my goodbyes to them, Seth cried for twenty minutes straight.

Josh, Luke and Joel also in their own ways showed their pain and confusion at having to say goodbye. I hated to leave them behind. But I had known that was part of the deal. And to be honest, it was starting to feel like a pretty raw deal. In Mark's gospel, Jesus promises to repay one-hundred-fold the people we give up for his sake, but how do you repay one-fold of a broken heart, never mind one-hundred-fold?

But Pete told me something else about his boys. It gives me hope that the pain is worthwhile.

'After seeing you go to Japan, both Josh and Seth are genuinely thinking through the possibility of dedicating their lives to overseas mission.'

This made me realise an important (and admittedly obvious) truth: children grow up.

This is painful because the cute little thing we adore slowly disappears, but also joyful because something, or rather someone, greater takes its place. It's still not fun, but now I know that whilst my departure to Japan means that I will miss seeing Seth grow up, it will also be part of the means for helping him grow.

He will learn (no doubt aided by his parents) about losing friends, the cost of missions – which is really just the cost of following Jesus – the sadness of bonds broken, the underlying brokenness of this world and the hope of redemption through the cross of Jesus. In other words, his worldview will change and grow. And as it does, so will Seth.

Saying goodbye to Seth felt like a sacrifice. But I've come to realise that actually you don't make sacrifices for the sake of Jesus. You make investments. Investments in your life, but also in the lives of others. Like all investments, there's a cost. But like all wise investments, the rewards are worth it.

And speaking of wisdom, once I arrived in Japan I realised I needed a lot of it. Mostly to answer a question that I somehow hadn't thought through before committing my life to mission in Japan: what is a missionary? And on top of that, am I one?

8

But am I a Missionary?

The second most common question I get asked in Japan is some form of, 'What do you do?' (The first is, 'Where are you from?' The third is, 'Why Japan?' And the fourth, 'Is your hair dyed?')

It's a tough question to answer.

I mostly go with something like, 'I work for a church.'

But that often gets the response, 'You're a priest?!'

It does lead to some fun conversations though, and I think it's the best answer I have going.

Because I don't really want to just say that I'm a missionary.

It's not that I think that's a wrong answer, or that being a missionary is a bad thing. It's probably the most correct answer in a lot of ways. But it also has the potential to make people think I'm a Mormon, especially with my light ginger hair (I prefer 'African Sunset' but somehow that hasn't caught on). We get a lot of Mormon and Jehovah's Witness missionaries in Japan, and it's confusing enough for people to know the difference between what we teach and practice without me accidentally telling people that I'm one of them.

But surely when I'm talking to Christians I can simply tell them I'm a missionary without causing such confusion? Well, yes and no. The thing is I don't really feel like a missionary. Not like a proper one anyway. I don't fit the mould very well. I can't play any musical instruments – a fact that has genuinely confused some Japanese Christians. I once made the mistake of trying to entertain some church kids by playing the one half-of-a-song that I know on the church piano and one of the members overheard it and then it took me a solid five minutes to convince them that I couldn't actually play piano and I really couldn't help out with the worship music.

I'm also not really keen on teaching English, which is another expectation I've encountered in Japan. When missionaries from Taiwan and Brazil are happy to run English classes, it really confuses people that I – a native speaker from the birthplace of English – don't want to. Sure I'll do some. But mostly I don't enjoy it. Except for kids' English camps, but that's because you just get to play games using English.

I suppose those wouldn't feel like big problems if I were a gifted evangelist, happy to go walking the streets and talking to strangers about Jesus in a natural and engaging way. But that's not me either. (I knew one exception to this standard missionary model, a Brazilian friend who also lacked musical skills and a passion for English teaching, but he could dance. And I have been told that I dance 'with the grace of a dying swan'.) I had come to Japan to serve the Japanese church, but when I arrived I couldn't see what I had to offer.

I was able to avoid these doubts for my first nine months as a missionary since I was studying Japanese full time. I had dreaded this. My experiences of Japanese classes back in the UK had been pretty rubbish. Mostly because I struggled to learn grammatical concepts like the difference between transitive and intransitive verbs. But somehow I found myself really enjoying my lessons at the language school in Sapporo. And more miraculously it seemed I wasn't rubbish at learning Japanese now. I was increasing in my ability to read, and becoming more and more confident in speaking. And with this my certainty that God had called me to Japan also grew. And yet, still my doubts remained.

It seemed unavoidable: if I was going to be a missionary then I would need to let go of my preferences and get into English-based outreach.

But then I made a discovery – or rather a rediscovery – that gave me a way to share the good news of Jesus while doing something that I really did love.

9

Rediscovering Ultimate

I love books almost as much as I love food. And I was enjoying my Japanese study. But I quickly realised that spending all my time in the library would drive me insane. Plus there's quite a difference between how men and women speak Japanese, and as most of the teachers at my school were women, there was a real danger that I would end up sounding like a Japanese housewife. I needed to practise speaking Japanese with men, which would mean finding some Japanese men.

Sports seemed like a natural way to get to meet guys my own age, but the question was, which sport?

Maybe I should get back into doing some martial arts? But I had officially reached 30 and despite promising myself that I wouldn't let it happen, I had become one of those people who made groaning noises when they stood up. And I don't mean standing up from being thrown to the ground. Just standing up in general. Also, Japan is famous for having low levels of crime. The idea of letting someone throw me onto the ground now just seemed daft: why get covered in bruises to learn to protect myself from an attack that would never happen?

Maybe baseball then? It is, after all, the most popular sport in Japan. Or football? Again, very popular. There was an indoor pitch down the road from the language and culture centre where I studied. A few other missionaries had joined in pickup games there and told me it was a great way to get to know people. The only problem was I hate football. This is probably not the place to explain why and how I hate it, but I do. But then again, maybe this was just one more of those things where I would have to die to my own wishes and embrace something I didn't like for the sake of the gospel.

I thought about Ultimate. I'd love to be able to get to know Japanese people whist playing Frisbee. To be honest, I'd just love to play Frisbee, even if I didn't get to make any friends through it. I had played a little bit whilst I was at Bible college, but only casual four-a-side pickup games with other students. I missed the buzz of tournaments. But God had called me to Japan. And I knew that would entail making sacrifices. I had tried to find an Ultimate Frisbee team when I was in Sendai for the year, but I soon discovered that it was even less known here than in the UK.

I was talking about this with one of my teachers and the next week he told me that he'd done some searching and discovered that a couple of the local universities had teams. He helped me write a polite email to each of them explaining that I was neither Japanese nor a student but keen to play. One replied to say that I was welcome to join in their practices on a Saturday morning. They already had a few *shakaijin* (non-students) who trained with them.

So a few days later I went down, dressed in my old university team kit, with directions to get to the training field. I walked through the gates, nodded politely to the security guard who stared politely back and starting looking for the Frisbee team. I made my way past the baseball pitch, through the American football fields and past the running track. I reached the edge of the campus to find my path blocked by a forest. I started to reread the instructions, and wondered which bit I had got wrong, when I heard an excited shout from somewhere in front of me. Looking through the gaps between the trees I could just make out the familiar shape of a Frisbee arching through the air. I was late for practice, but at least I'd found it.

I fought my way through the forest (on the way home I discovered there was a path) and came out on the edge of the backup baseball pitch, bringing a throwing drill to a brief stop. I quickly booted-up and ran to join the line, bowing my apology for being late. Formal introductions would have to wait until after the drill was finished. I stuttered a simple greeting to the person in front of me. I suddenly felt all the nervousness of being at Frisbee training for the first time combined with being new to Japan. I was desperate to make a good first impression. It was a basic backhand 'run, catch, throw, repeat' drill. So obviously I dropped my first pass. The disc bounced away from me. I dived after it, catching it just before crashing into the ground. I heard a cheer behind me, and a squeal just above me. I looked up to see the team manager that I had just nearly dived into, hugging a clipboard and shaking a little bit. Not quite the first impression I was hoping for. But at least I caught the disc.

Thankfully the rest of the training went on without me terrifying anyone else, and they invited me to keep coming. Bit by bit my Ultimate Frisbee muscle memory came back to me. And as I'd hoped I also picked up Japanese phrases that weren't in the textbooks. Phrases like *donmai*, a brilliant abbreviation of 'don't worry, never mind'. But best of all I got to know a bunch of folk who shared my love for Ultimate Frisbee.

A few months later I was at my first Ultimate tournament in Japan. With Ultimate being such a minor sport it's tough to find sports fields to use for training, but for tournaments where we need a dozen pitches you have to go quite rural.

And so we headed to Fuji Town – a small town in Japan that, as you've probably guessed, is close to Japan's most famous mountain. We arrived at the pitches greeted by grey clouds and light drizzle, but after our first game as we sat huddled under our team gazebo, sharing bananas and banter, the clouds gave way to reveal Mount Fuji, in all its glory rising above us.

Japanese people proudly claim Mount Fuji as the most beautiful mountain in the world. As I took photos of people jumping after Frisbees with the mountain in the background I decided I agreed. And then almost as if it were the next logical step I decided on three more things. First, I loved Japan. Second, I loved Ultimate Frisbee. And third, I wanted to use Frisbee to share Jesus with the Japanese.

I offered up a short prayer, explaining my feelings to God and praising him for creating Mount Fuji and Frisbees. I asked for him to guide me and help me to share his love with these people who shared my love for Frisbee. It was really the only thing that I had in common with them, but I was confident that for God that was enough. I felt sure that he would use me as

I was, but I had no idea how. It was exciting and scary. But it felt ... right. It felt natural, like this was what I was meant to do. I wondered, maybe this was what it meant to be a missionary.

Over the coming months and years I kept playing Ultimate as much as I could. Sometimes I would get opportunities to talk to people about the gospel. Often I would learn new things about Japanese culture. Mostly I enjoyed running around after plastic discs with my friends who just happened to be Japanese.

And then I turned 32 and one of my friends asked me if I would like to go to France with the Japanese mixed team. It didn't take me long to decide that yes, I would love to go.

10

Jesus Uses Throwaway-ers

Now there's something I need to clarify. You might be thinking, 'Wow, if Levi was on the Japanese national team he must be pretty good at Ultimate Frisbee'. But you'd be wrong. I am incredibly average. And I'm not being humble, just honest. I mean, I am quick. I can outrun most people in the over-thirties bracket. I can get into space and catch the disc. But I have one major weakness: I throwaway ... a lot.

See, in Ultimate Frisbee once you catch or pick up the disc you have to throw it. You can't just hand it to someone on your team who can throw. So when I get the disc I throw. But often I do one of two things. I either panic and throw an impossible-to-catch pass to nobody in particular. Or, I'm over-confident and throw an impossible-to-catch pass to nobody in particular. In other words I throw the Frisbee away. I become what you could call a 'throwaway-er'.

And not just on the pitch. As a missionary I also quite often throw away gospel opportunities. Someone shows interest in spiritual matters but I get afraid of offending them so I move the conversation on to TV or something equally safe. Somebody asks me a question about Jesus being the only way to God and I end up saying something vague and non-committal. I see an old lady get onto my packed train and I know that I should give her my seat, but I'm tired and want to read. And whilst I'm arguing with myself about whether I should stand up, someone else offers their seat. And I watch the lady start talking to them, wishing I wasn't so selfish.

But then I remember the stories of the Bible and remember that Jesus came for the throwaways and the throwaway-ers. He uses us in our failures. He works through our panicked drops and our pride-induced throwaways. Some of God's best work has been through incredibly average people like me.

When I was younger, one of my friends was getting baptised and I mentioned to him that I was kind of jealous because he was experiencing God's grace in a fresh new way that you only get when you first become a Christian.

He looked at me very confused, 'What are you talking about? You've had years more than me of enjoying the gospel. I'm looking forward to when I know as much of God's grace as you do now!'

He was right, of course. As heart-stoppingly amazing as it was to first dwell on the fact that Jesus would forgive someone like me, recently I have been even more amazed that he would not only rescue me from my rebellion but that he would use me (and keep using me!) to demonstrate his grace to others, despite the fact that I continually throwaway those opportunities. That I continue to be proud and petty, quick to anger and slow to forgive. That I persist in being totally underserving of his favour.

Because this hasn't been a story about me. I hope that is obvious. It's a story about Jesus and his incredible, unstoppable, amazing, ultimate grace.

Postscript: Run, Son, Run!

When I was in high school I got into running. It was my dad who really inspired me to do it. He was a super keen runner, training regularly and even running marathons occasionally. We would take strange routes home from town so he could hide bottles of water along the route that he would run later that evening.

I hadn't got to that level of commitment, but I did enjoy running. So when I found out that my school was organising a fun run, I entered straight away. A couple of my friends from school found out that I had entered and decided that they would be quicker than me. They entered too and soon the fun run had become, for us at least, a serious race.

The route was quite simple: we would start at the school, run out of the gates, along the nearby stream and then loop back next to the road, and back into the school grounds, around the sports fields and finish on the running track. I had worked out my strategy: get out in front, and then keep a steady pace, then I would save a little bit of energy for a final sprint finish down the last 100 metres of the running track.

My dad, who had come along to support me, had a similar idea. Except that he had decided on a different spot for when I should start sprinting.

I got out in front as I had wanted to do and by the time I was coming up to the school fields I had a comfortable lead. All was going to plan. Then I turned onto the fields and saw my dad waiting for me.

As soon as he saw me, he started screaming, 'Run! Run, son, run!'

I jumped in shock and starting running faster out of reflex. But then I realised there was still about 600 metres to go: far too long a distance to sprint. I started to slow down back to my jogging speed.

My dad didn't accept that.

'What are you doing? Don't slow down. Run!' And then unexpectedly (that is, even more unexpected than the shouting in general) he added, 'He's right behind you! Run! Run, son, run!'

Who was right behind me? I was pretty certain that nobody had been anywhere close to me. I went to see who it was.

'Don't look! Just run! He's catching you. Run, son, run!'

So I did. I went full out. I had no idea who it was that was closing in on me, but there was no way I was going to be overtaken so close to the finish line. I ran as fast as I could. And every time I started to flag, my dad, sprinting alongside me, would start shouting again.

'Run, son, run!'

I got onto the final stretch. My hopes of confidently crossing the line to the cheers of onlookers were shattered. First because I was now a sweating, snorting mess, half sprinting half staggering towards the finish line. And second because my dad was so focused on screaming at me to keep running that he was paying zero attention to the other parents and teachers stood waiting along the track like normal people. People were having to dive out of the way of my dad as he charged through the crowd, continuing his cheer: 'Run, son, run!'

I collapsed over the finish line, utterly exhausted. And then I remembered that I needed to get out of the way for whoever it was that had been so close to overtaking me. I rolled to the side and sat up, looking back down the track.

Nobody. There was no one there. I struggled to my feet, half-aware of my dad jumping and cheering to the side, and scanned the field. Nobody. There had been no one closing in on me. No reason for me to sprint the final half-mile of the race.

I learned two important lessons that day. First, don't trust my dad without question. And second, when you stop wondering and worrying about what's behind you and focus on the goal ahead, you can run faster and further than you thought possible.

I arrived in Japan to start my full-time ministry with OMF in June 2014. Six weeks later my dad fell from some scaffolding and went into hospital with a head injury. At first he was stable, and I thought he would recover. But then suddenly his condition got worse and he was put on life-support. I booked the earliest plane ticket I could back to England. It wasn't soon enough. The day I was due to fly I got a phone call from my sister. There was nothing they could do and they needed to turn off the life-support. I said goodbye to my dad over the phone, unsure whether he was able to hear me or not, and headed for the airport.

After the funeral I asked my mum whether she wanted me to stay in the UK. She told me that my dad was proud of me going to Japan and that he would have wanted me to return. I knew she was right. Whether it was a fun run or my calling as a missionary, my dad had always been supportive to the point of embarrassment. I could still hear him shouting at me, 'Run, son, run!'

I still do. And it keeps me going when I feel like giving up. When I'm tempted to slow down, to coast, to look back, to lose focus, to stop running.

And, of course, it's not just my dad. There are many great men and women of faith who have encouraged, and continue to encourage me, to keep running the race. To keep my eyes fixed forward. To keep my eyes fixed on Jesus. That's been the purpose of this book. Not that I would make myself out to be a great man of faith, but that by seeing the grace that God has poured onto my life, you will be encouraged to give your life fully to him. And my prayer is that wherever God leads you, you will always be able to hear the sound of your heavenly Father running alongside you, cheering for you with all his glorious might: 'Run, child, run!'

> *Therefore, since we are surrounded by such a great cloud of witnesses, let us throw off everything that hinders and the sin that so easily entangles. And let us run with perseverance the race marked out for us, fixing our eyes on Jesus, the pioneer and perfecter of faith. For the joy that was set before him he endured the cross, scorning its shame, and sat*

down at the right hand of the throne of God. Consider him who endured such opposition from sinners, so that you will not grow weary and lose heart (Hebrews 12:1-3).

We hope you've enjoyed Levi's story of his journey to Japan and how God has used his unusual skills.

Levi serves with OMF International, which was founded by James Hudson Taylor in 1865 as the China Inland Mission.

Today around 1,400 workers from 40 countries serve across East Asia. Their ministries vary from church planting to medical work and sport to theological education. But each of them seeks to serve the Church and share the good news of Jesus Christ in all its fullness.

Heart for Asia. Hope for Billions.

Find out more about OMF, check out our podcast and more free resources at:
omf.org/uk

/omfinternationaluk

omf_uk

omf_int

Ultimate
GRACE
Levi Booth

10 Publishing
a division of 10 of those.com